Jack the Brave

Written by Cyndie Kieffer

Illustrated by Monique Romischer

Copyright © 2020 Cyndie Kieffer
Illustrated by Monique Romischer
All rights reserved.

No part of this book may be reproduced in any manner without the written consent of the publisher except for brief excerpts in critical reviews or articles.

ISBN: 978-1-61244-858-9
Library of Congress Control Number: 2020909682

Printed in the United States of America

Halo Publishing International
8000 W Interstate 10
Suite 600
San Antonio, Texas 78230
www.halopublishing.com
contact@halopublishing.com

This book is dedicated to my most perfect Jack, who inspires me to be brave and also to Dennis, who always catches me when I fall.

Hi, my name is Jack. I am a Border Collie, and I like to herd things and keep everything in order.

My mom and dad love me so much. They make sure I have plenty of healthy food and toys. My favorite toy is a purple squeak ball!

I am a therapy dog. I like to make people happy and make them feel better when they are sad. I even work with my mommy.

I have a brother Colton, another named Norm, who is a cool guy, and a sister Dori. I love them all, although sometimes I try to get Dori in trouble.

I love being a therapy dog! My mom and I go to all sorts of fun places. I also love meeting new people.

Mommy and I have to be evaluated every two years so we can keep visiting people. This just means someone has us take a test to show that we still are doing everything right and that I still love what I do.

Part of how Mommy and Daddy show that they love me is making sure I am healthy. I go to see my veterinarian, a doctor for animals. I love everyone there. They give me snacks and tell me that I am cute.

One time I went and they said that I needed a tooth pulled so Mommy made an appointment to take me back.

The day my doctor pulled my tooth she noticed a tumor on me. She told my mommy that it might be something to check on to make sure I was healthy. This scared my mommy.

Mommy was crying and my Auntie Dusty hugged us both to make us feel better.

Mommy got a phone call from my doctor. My doctor told her that I had cancer and needed to see a different kind of doctor. Mommy made an appointment for me to see a veterinarian at the University of Illinois.

Mommy told me I had cancer. She said that cancer happens when sick cells keep growing inside someone's body. They grow so much they take over where healthy cells are supposed to be in the body. Mommy said I would have surgery to take out the tumor. She told me to be brave because they would do everything they could to make me healthy.

I kept working and playing...and being brave.

Mommy, Daddy and I went to a big hospital. We met a nice doctor who told us what needed to happen to make me feel better.

Mommy looked worried. I let her know that it will be ok and that I am brave. Brave means doing something even though we are scared. Sometimes it is hard to be brave and I have to think of the things I did that were scary. I learned how to herd ducks and that was kind of scary because they made a funny noise at me. I learned how to jump and run in agility. That was scary because I didn't want to get hurt. It was also scary when I took my first Pet Partner test. I did all of those things even though they were scary.

After the surgery, I had to wear a cone so I wouldn't tear out my stitches. I hated that cone. The doctors said they got all of the tumor out and now I have to rest and get better. I hate resting almost as much as the cone.

One morning I woke up and didn't feel good. I didn't want to eat. I just wanted to be held. My tummy hurt really badly.

Mommy called the doctor and we went back to the hospital. I had to stay there a few days to get better this time. Mommy told me to be brave. It was hard to be brave, but I kept trying. I thought about my mommy and that made me feel better. She made sure that my purple squeak ball and favorite blanket were with me all the time.

I was able to go home after a few days. I kept getting stronger and I finished three chemotherapy treatments. I was brave every time. My mommy was always there. All of the doctors were nice to me and wanted me to be happy.

My hair started falling out. When it grew back some of it was red like my sister Dori's hair.

After my last chemotherapy treatment, Mommy took me out to celebrate. I ate a steak! It was so good!

I got to go back to work. I saw all of my friends. Everyone told me I had been a very brave boy.

I was able to play with Colton and Dori whenever I wanted. I could also go visit people with my buddy, Baxter.

After someone has cancer they go see a doctor a lot. Just to be sure everything is ok. I always like to visit people in the waiting room when I am there to see my doctor. Sometimes they are sad or worried and I try to cheer them up.

Mommy says I am very brave to take care of everyone even though I am somewhere I don't want to be.

Once I had my one-year checkup, Mommy decided to take me to a really special place. It was a cancer center for people. Mommy said it was a way for us to cheer people up and help them be brave just like me.

I still visit there every month. I want to make the nurses smile and I want the people to know that they can be brave when they are scared...just like I was.

Information for professionals and parents regarding cancer diagnosis and how children are impacted:

Cancer is scary for everyone; adults and children alike. It is important to talk about the diagnosis sooner rather than later as waiting to talk about it can cause issues regarding trust. Some people prefer to plan out what they want to say or even practice beforehand. Remember the adage, "it isn't what you say but how you say it" in this circumstance. Try to speak in a calm voice and don't become frustrated with yourself if you start to cry. Crying is an appropriate response and lets the child know that it is okay to cry.

Give the child a chance to ask questions and speak using words that your child understands. Often using simple and concrete sentences is best. It might also be beneficial to let the child know that this happened on its own--nobody caused the cancer. Children need to know that cancer is not contagious as well. Providing reassurance to the child that they are loved and will be cared for is important as they are likely frightened by this news. Additionally, explaining that there will be changes in the daily routine ahead of time will help children adjust.

Cancer impacts everyone and each person responds to this differently. It is best to keep your child's personality, developmental stage and needs in mind during these discussions.

Jack

www.ingramcontent.com/pod-product-compliance
Lightning Source LLC
Chambersburg PA
CBHW041439040426
42453CB00021B/2460